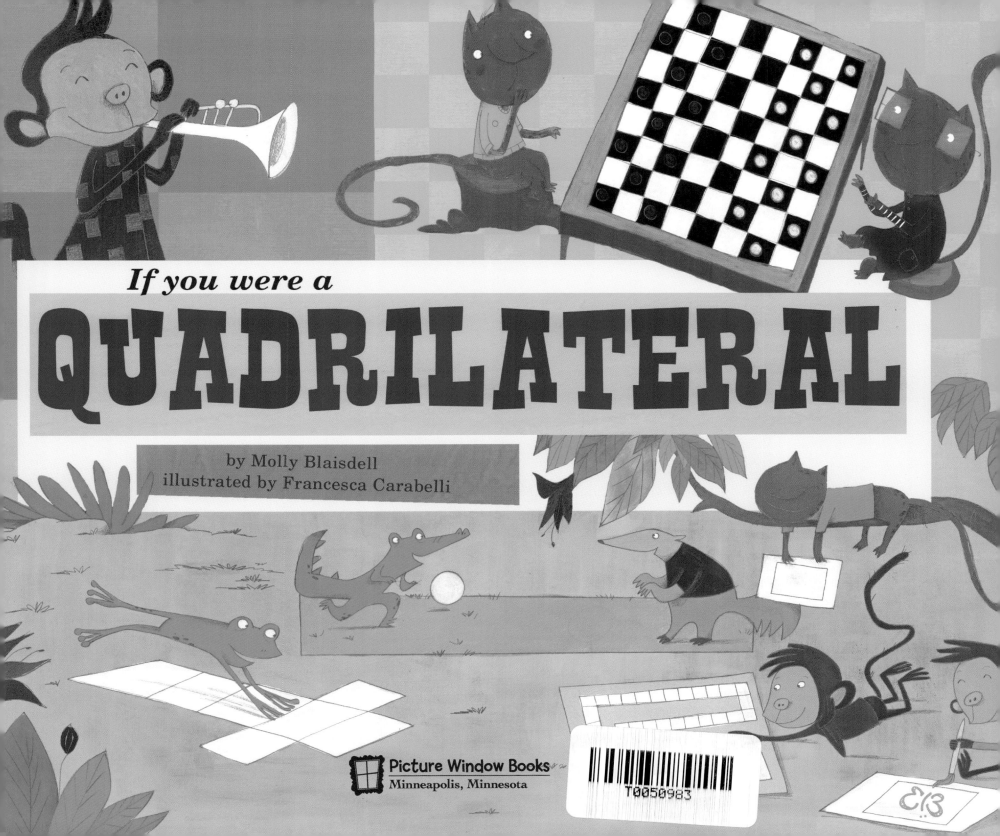

If you were a
QUADRILATERAL

by Molly Blaisdell
illustrated by Francesca Carabelli

Picture Window Books
Minneapolis, Minnesota

T0050983

Editor: Jill Kalz
Designer: Lori Bye
Page Production: Melissa Kes
Art Director: Nathan Gassman
Editorial Director: Nick Healy
Creative Director: Joe Ewest
The illustrations in this book were created with watercolor and gouache.

Picture Window Books
A Capstone Imprint
1710 Roe Crest Drive
North Mankato, MN 56003
www.capstonepub.com

Library of Congress Cataloging-in-Publication Data
Blaisdell, Molly, 1964-
If you were a quadrilateral / by Molly Blaisdell ; illustrated by Francesca Carabelli.
p. cm. — (Math fun)
Includes index.
ISBN 978-1-4048-5511-3 (library binding)
ISBN 978-1-4048-5690-5 (paperback)
1. Quadrilaterals—Juvenile literature. 2. Shapes—Juvenile literature. I. Carabelli, Francesca, ill. II. Title.
QA482.B57 2010
516'.154—dc22
2009006890

Special thanks to our adviser for his expertise:

Stuart Farm, M.Ed., Mathematics Lecturer
University of North Dakota

Printed in the United States   5863

If you were a quadrilateral ...

... you would make playtime lots of fun.

If you were a quadrilateral, you would be a flat, closed figure with four sides. All your sides would be straight.

The animals love to paint.
They love painting quadrilaterals most of all.

If you were a quadrilateral, you would be a polygon with four sides. A polygon is a closed figure with three or more straight sides.

1st Prize

Polygon Art Contest

Mariana hangs her picture on the wall.
She hopes she wins.
First prize is a new set of paints!

If you were a quadrilateral, you would have four angles.
An angle is the measurement between two sides at a corner.

The bases are loaded.
The Terrific Toucans need one more run to win!
Luiz gets ready to swing.

If you were a quadrilateral, you could be a rectangle. Each pair of opposite sides would be the same length. All your angles would be the same size.

Alice plays tennis with Ana.
Neither one of them plays well.
But they both have a blast!

If you were a quadrilateral, you could be a square. Your sides would all be the same length. Your angles would all be the same size, too.

Bruna plays checkers with Lucas.

They place all their pieces on the black squares.

If you were a quadrilateral, you could be a rhombus. Your sides would all be the same length. Each pair of opposite angles would be the same size. A square is a type of rhombus. But rhombuses can take many shapes.

Pedro's band practices every day.

One day, the Rowdy Rhombuses will be famous!

If you were a quadrilateral, you could be part of a special family called parallelograms. Each pair of opposite sides would be the same length. The opposite sides would also never touch or cross each other. They would be parallel. Squares, rectangles, and rhombuses are all types of parallelograms.

Camila and her family work out at the gym.
They stretch, lift weights, and tumble on mats
shaped like parallelograms.

If you were a quadrilateral, you could be a trapezoid. Only two of your sides would be parallel to one another.

Everyone grabs a kite and races up the hill. Last one up is a rotten egg!

21

You could fly high in the sky ...

... if you were a quadrilateral.

DRAWING QUADRILATERALS

What you need:

paper   a few friends
pens or pencils   a timer

What you do:

Give each person a sheet of paper and a pen or pencil. Timing yourselves for one minute, look around the room and draw as many quadrilaterals as you can find. Award one point for each parallelogram. Award five points for each quadrilateral that is *not* a parallelogram. Who got the highest score?

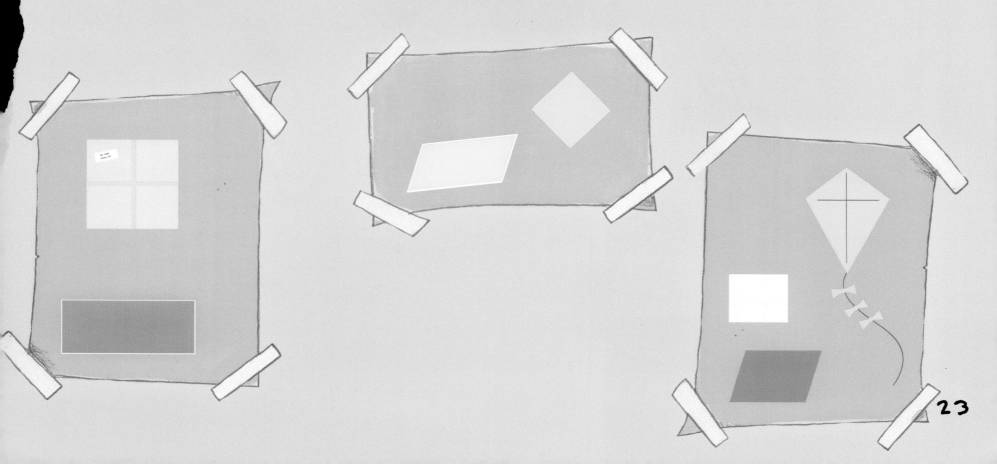

Glossary

angle—the measurement between two sides at a corner

parallel—the same distance apart at all points and never touching or crossing

parallelogram—a quadrilateral with equal opposite sides that are parallel

polygon—a flat, closed figure with three or more straight sides

quadrilateral—a flat, closed figure with four straight sides

rectangle—a quadrilateral with four right angles

rhombus—a quadrilateral with four equal sides and equal opposite angles

square—a quadrilateral with four equal sides and four right angles

trapezoid—a quadrilateral with one pair of parallel sides

To Learn More

More Books to Read

Friedman, Mel, and Ellen Weiss. *Kitten Castle.* New York: Kane Press, 2001.

Sarfatti, Esther. *Shapes. Squares.* Vero Beach, Fla.: Rourke Pub., 2008.

Internet Sites

FactHound offers a safe, fun way to find Internet sites related to this book. All of the sites on FactHound have been researched by our staff.

Here's all you do:
Visit www.facthound.com
FactHound will fetch the best sites for you!

Index

Look for all of the books in the Math Fun series

If You Were a Circle

If You Were a Divided-by Sign

If You Were a Fraction

If You Were a Minus Sign

If You Were a Minute

If You Were a Plus Sign

If You Were a Polygon

If You Were a Pound or a Kilogram

If You Were a Quadrilateral

If You Were a Quart or a Liter

If You Were a Set

If You Were a Times Sign

If You Were a Triangle

If You Were an Even Number

If You Were an Inch or a Centimeter

If You Were an Odd Number